The Gospel of Mark for Little Ones

Written By
Sara Beth Meyer, MTh

Illustrated By
Allison Hsu, MD

The Gospel of Mark for Little Ones
© 2023 Sara Beth Meyer, MTh, and Allison Hsu, MD. All rights reserved.

Available from:
Marian Helpers Center
Stockbridge, MA 01263

Prayerline: 1-800-804-3823
Orderline: 1-800-462-7426
Website: ShopMercy.org

Library of Congress Control Number: 2023935915
ISBN: 978-1-59614-594-8

Imprimi Potest:
Very Rev. Chris Alar, MIC
Provincial Superior
The Blessed Virgin Mary, Mother of Mercy Province
April 25, 2023
Feast of St. Mark, Evangelist

Nihil Obstat:
Robert A. Stackpole, STD
Censor Deputatus
April 25, 2023

Printed in the United States of America

MARIAN PRESS
STOCKBRIDGE MA 01263

For my brother, C. John,
and for all who participate in the suffering of
our Lord each day with undimmed faith.
For as Christ's sufferings overflow to us,
so through Christ does our encouragement also overflow.
(2 Corinthians 1:5)

– *Sara*

For all my Little Ones:
Sophia, Monica, and Olivia, Carter,
and also Hannah, Kian, Madison,
P.J., Bridget, Gianna,
and Theodore.

– *Allison*

About the Authors

Sara Beth Meyer holds a bachelor's degree in education and a master's degree in theology. She enjoys writing articles, books, and songs about faith and family, and is thrilled to collaborate with Allison on both *The Gospel of Matthew for Little Ones* and *The Gospel of Mark for Little Ones*, especially now that her nine children have begun welcoming Little Ones of their own. She can be found at SaraBethMeyer.com.

Allison Hsu holds a degree in medicine and is an award-winning artist. She is a wife, mother, and illustrator of *The Gospel of Matthew for Little Ones*, *The Gospel of Mark for Little Ones*, and the *Little Ones* newsletter. She enjoys using the gift of craftsmanship and sketching the little things of life with great love. She can also be found at SaraBethMeyer.com.

Acknowledgments

We thank everyone who field-tested and gave feedback during the creation phase, the folks at Marian Press who partnered with us in the publication of *The Gospel of Mark for Little Ones*, and the Immaculate Heart of Mary, under whose protection we place this entire project.

John lived in the desert, wearing only camel hair.

He made a way for Jesus, baptizing sinners there.

One day Jesus came to him, to be baptized, too.

The Father said, "Beloved Son"; the Spirit: down He flew!

Jesus went into the wild, alone to pray and fast.

Forty days passed by, and then Satan came at last.

Our Lord could not be tempted by the things he had to say.

Jesus had no time for lies and drove that foe away.

Jesus went to fishermen who worked hard on the sea.

To Andrew, Simon, James, & John, He said, "Come after Me."

They followed Him throughout the land and saw Him heal and preach.

He cured the sick and healed the lame, for all were in His reach.

In a house where Jesus taught, it got too full to enter.   *Mark 2*

To help their friend, men lowered him right into the center.

Jesus healed the man from sin who came down through the roof.

Then He had him rise and walk, since doubters needed proof.

Jesus called some other friends to share His way of love.   *Mark 3*

His words were new and strange to hear: a message from above.

Some people became angry. They said He should behave.

But Jesus had to heal the sick; for these He came to save.

One day when Jesus' family just wanted Him alone,

Away from all the crowds of folks whose faith in Him had grown,

He said that everyone could be His mother, sister, brother.

Every person only had to love God and each other!

He taught the people stories, showing God knows all their needs.   *Mark 4*

He said their faith could grow and grow, like plants from tiny seeds.

Jesus said our faith's a lamp. It should be kept so bright.

He even calmed the sea by faith, one dark and stormy night.

One day a crowd pushed into Him. A lady who was sickly   *Mark 5*

Got close enough to touch His clothes, and she was healed so quickly.

Later, Jesus went to heal a little girl who died.

He took her hand, and so she rose and walked right by His side!

Jesus went to preach one day, back in His native land.   *Mark 6*

People who had known Him said that He was not so grand.

Jesus could not help the people who would not believe.

He just healed some folks and said that it was time to leave.

He sent His friends to preach and heal. They all went two by two.

They came back astonished by the things that they could do.

God had them drive out demons and anoint the sick with oil.

Jesus said to stay where asked, as payment for their toil.

Jesus and His group of friends went off to rest a bit.

Crowds of thousands flocked to them and wouldn't let them sit.

Jesus preached a while and knew that they all had to eat.

With one boy's loaves and fish, He fed 5,000: what a feat!

Jesus sent the people and His twelve friends all away.

He knew He needed time alone with God to end His day.

The twelve men got into a boat. They rowed against the breeze.

Jesus walked right up to them, on water, with such ease!

Leaders taught that to be clean, just wash your face and hands. *Mark 7*

Jesus said God knows the heart, and He understands:

Sin doesn't come from using dirty hands or bowls or beds.

Evil grows in angry hearts and thoughts inside our heads.

A stranger came to Him one day to get help for her child.

Jesus said He wasn't sent for her, but all the while …

The mother knew that He could help and wouldn't dare to leave

Until He said the girl was cured, because the mom believed.

Some people brought a man to Him who couldn't speak or hear.

Jesus took him from the crowd, to heal his tongue and ears.

The more that Jesus did for them, the more that His fame grew.

Everyone kept telling all the great things He could do!

One day Jesus asked His friends who people said He was. *Mark 8*

With all the healings He'd performed, the folks were all a-buzz:

Was He a famous prophet who had come back from the dead?

"Who do you say that I am?" "The Messiah," Peter said.

Our Lord explained that He had come to suffer, die, and rise.

He knew they didn't understand. The shock shown in their eyes.

He said they must pick up their cross each day and suffer strife.

This was the only way that led to everlasting life.

Jesus brought three of His friends up to a mountain's height. *Mark 9*

Peter, James, & John all saw His clothes go dazzling white.

Suddenly Elijah came with Moses by his side.

The Father's voice was heard again. The three were terrified.

11

They came down the mountainside, and then Jesus said

Not to share the vision 'til His rising from the dead.

Peter, James, & John all knew the sight was Heaven-sent.

Even so, they didn't understand what all it meant.

When they rejoined their other friends, they saw a man whose son

Was hurt and needed Jesus' help to ever have some fun.

He begged our Lord to heal the boy and felt doubt in His grief.

Jesus healed when Dad cried out, "Help my unbelief!"

One day on a journey, all His friends began to fight:

Who'd rule in the Kingdom? Who'd have the most might?

He embraced a child, then explained so tenderly,

"Who … receives one child … receives the One who sent me."

The friends still didn't understand what Jesus meant to say, *Mark 10*

So when some kids came up to Him, the men pushed them away.

Our Lord grew very angry at His friends, as all could see.

He blessed the kids, instructing, "Let the children come to Me."

He started on a journey, when a rich man came and asked,

What must be done for Heaven, for he would do any task!

Keeping all commandments, he thought God must be so glad.

When Jesus said give all and come, he went away, so sad.

Jesus told the people that the rich would struggle so.

Trusting in their money was just not the way to go.

Peter felt dismayed: they had left all that they knew.

Jesus promised lots of blessings … and eternal life, too!

Our Lord came to Jerusalem, and said there would be tied

A new white colt just waiting there. He'd be the first to ride.

His twelve friends brought it to Him. He was greeted by a crowd

Who waved palms and sang, "Hosanna!" They were so joyful and loud.

Our Lord approached the Temple, and His heart began to grieve

That men outside weren't prayerful. They were like a den of thieves.

He overturned the tables, so their piles of money spilled.

Officials started wondering how they could have Him killed.

A scribe came asking Jesus which commandment was the best.

Jesus said that just one thing was prized above the rest:

Love God with heart, soul, mind, and strength, and neighbor as yourself.

Their short talk had said it all. The crowd asked nothing else.

One day, Jesus told His friends that they should give with trust

When men came to the treasury, as they knew they must.

Each one gave lots of money. They were truly wealthy gents.

Jesus said a widow offered more with her few cents.

His friends asked when the world would end. Could it be close at hand? *Mark 13*

He said they shouldn't worry; share God's love in every land.

He told them not to listen to false teaching when they hear it.

Rather, they should let their hearts be guided by the Spirit.

When Passover approached, He knew His dying was in sight. *Mark 14*

He told the twelve that He would be betrayed that very night.

They were shocked and wondered who could have this evil wish.

He looked at Judas as they dipped their bread into the dish.

For the special meal, our Lord took bread and blessing cup,

Praying in thanksgiving as He lifted them both up.

The bread became His Body and the cup, His Blood soon shed.

He said it was His last meal 'til He'd risen from the dead.

Jesus told them they'd all scatter in the hours to come.

Peter swore his loyalty; he wouldn't be like some.

Jesus said to Peter that he would deny Him thrice.

It wouldn't take too long — just before the cock crows twice.

He went into a garden and took Peter, James, & John.

Jesus asked them all to pray, but they slept on and on.

He prayed to God to let the awful suffering pass by …

But if it was the Father's will, He would in love soon die.

A mob burst in the garden, all holding club and sword.

Judas signaled who to seize by kissing our dear Lord.

Why did they need weapons? Jesus always taught in peace.

No one came to help, when He was brought to the high priest.

A council met to question Him and see if He should die.

They called all sorts of witnesses, and many tried to lie.

Jesus stood there silently, as peaceful as a lamb.

"Are you the Messiah?" He agreed, "I am."

They yelled at Jesus, hitting Him, while Peter stood outside.

When asked if he knew Jesus, Peter three times lied.

All the while, a rooster crowed; the prophecy was kept.

Peter knew what he had done. He felt so sad, he wept.

They brought our Lord to Pilate, the leader at that time.

Mark 15

Pilate wondered why. He was guilty of no crime.

He knew it was their envy that made them act so proudly.

They stirred the people all to shout "Crucify Him!" loudly.

Soldiers tortured Jesus and put thorns upon His head.

Then they nailed Him to a cross, to hang there until dead.

Jesus never cried for help. The soldiers found it odd.

When He died, one realized, "This man was the Son of God."

Joseph, a rich councilman, did something very brave:

He offered his own tomb to bury Jesus, as His grave.

They wrapped Him up and left Him in the rock tomb all alone,

Then sealed the entrance to the cave with a massive stone.

Three women went to Jesus' tomb at sunrise that Sunday.   *Mark 16*

They were surprised to see the heavy stone just rolled away.

One of them, named Mary, saw Him risen from the dead.

She ran to tell His friends that it had happened like He said.

His friends would not believe her, for they just did not seem able.

So Jesus came to them Himself, all seated at a table.

He knew they were confused and sad; they still had to grieve.

Even so, He told His friends that they should all believe.

Jesus said to go and share the Good News without shame,

to drive out demons, heal the sick, all in Jesus' Name.

Our Lord returned to Heaven, to His Father up above.

Now we all can pray to Him to help us share God's love!

About The Gospel of Mark for Little Ones

In Mark 9 & 10, Jesus explains to His disciples that they must become like little children to enter the Kingdom of Heaven. How can **we** grow in childlike trust? We can be generous like the boy in Mark 6, whose food is the means of a miracle. We can be persistent like the mother in Mark 7, and honest about our short-comings like the father in Mark 9; in both cases, the childlike faith of the parents prompts Jesus to heal their children.

May we grow in faith, hope, and love each day, trusting in our Father at all times and following our brother Jesus all the way home.

Jesus prayed the Psalms! Ask Jesus to help you learn these verses about trust by heart:

Offer fitting sacrifices and trust in the Lord.   Psalm 4:6

Trust in the Lord and do good that you may dwell in the land and live secure.
                                                                              Psalm 37:3

Better to take refuge in the Lord than to put one's trust in mortals.   Psalm 118:85